The Little Maths Song Games

by Sally Featherstone

Illustrations by
Sally Featherstone

LITTLE BOOKS WITH BIG IDEAS

Reprinted 2010
Published 2009 by A&C Black Publishers Limited
36 Soho Square, London W1D 3QY
www.acblack.com

First published in the UK by Featherstone Education, 2002

ISBN 978-1-9041-8732-5

Text © Sally Featherstone
Illustrations © Sally Featherstone

A CIP record for this publication is available from
the British Library.

All rights reserved. No part of this publication may be reproduced
in any form or by any means – graphic, electronic, or mechanical,
including photocopying, recording, taping or information storage
or retrieval systems – without the prior permission in writing
of the publishers.

Printed in Great Britain by Latimer Trend & Company Limited.

This book is produced using paper that is made from wood grown
inmanaged, sustainable forests. It is natural, renewable and
recyclable.The logging and manufacturing processes conform to
the environmental regulations of the country of origin.

**To see our full range of titles
visit www.acblack.com**

Contents

Introduction		4 – 7
Pass it On	The Number Ring	8 – 9
Splat the Number	Ten Little numbers	10 – 11
Find the Shape	The Feely Box	12 – 13
Play that Number	We Can Count on the Tambourine	14 – 15
Junk Numbers	One Finger, One Thumb	16 – 17
Through the Arches	Ten Little Racing Cars	18 – 19
Big Races	Count to Five	20 – 21
Grab and Guess	Grab and Guess	22 – 23
Button Toss	The Button Song	24 – 25
Spot the Dots	This Old Man	26 – 27
Under the Cup	The Busy Workmen	28 – 29
Skittles	Roll a Ball	30 – 31
Hide and Find	The Helpers	32 – 33
Lotto	Playing Lotto	34 – 35
Turn 2, Match 2	One, Two, Buckle my Shoe	36 – 37
Big Numbers	Count in Tens	38 – 39
Only 2 More Days	The Months	40 – 41
Let's Pretend	Serving	42 – 43
Snap a Shape	Finding Pairs	44 – 45
Penny Exchange	The Penny Game	46 – 47
Button Your Coat	Button Up	48 – 49
Up The Ladder	The Ladder	50 – 51
Hop, Skip and Jump	Keep it Moving	52 – 53
Number Spot	Ten Little Teddies	54 – 55
Go Fish!	1, 2, 3, 4, 5	56 – 57
Step and Squeeze	Stepping and Squeezing	58 – 59
Think of a Number	Counting Backwards	60 – 61
In the Hoop You Go!	The Sorting Song	62 – 63
Blindfold	Counting Blindfold	64 – 65
Button Sort and cards for the game		66 – 67
Pictures for Pairs Game		68 – 70

Introduction

The games and songs in this book will all support your children in learning about numbers and counting; but as we all know, children never learn one thing at a time! While they play the games and sing the songs, they will also be developing personal and social skills. Games require patience, turn taking, negotiation and coping with the disappointment of losing. Games are also one of the best ways of developing conversational language.

We have always known that young children learn by doing, by being active and by using their bodies. We now have the scientific evidence that whole body activity actually develops children's brains, building links and connections that reinforce what they are learning. The more senses children use and the more of their bodies are active, the more they will remember.

The Games

The games in the book are all suitable for small groups, and many can be adapted for larger groups or whole classes. Almost all the games can be played indoors or out, and some are particularly suited to playing in the garden. Below the title on each page, you will see the focus of the game; this will help you, when you are planning your work, to link the games to your maths focus for the week or the day.

Each game has a list of the things you need to find or make. Most of them use equipment or materials you will already have, or can easily collect. Much of the equipment can be made by the children themselves, with your help, thus increasing their sense of involvement and encouraging them to be independent. Make the preparation stage an activity in itself, starting the session at the craft or technology table and then moving into playing the game.

All the games are intended for children in the Early Years Foundation Stage. However, some will need simplifying for the youngest children and some will need to use higher numbers for the older, more mature children. Use your professional judgement when choosing which game to play and at which level you will play it.

Remember that younger children need a longer time to think during games, and their concentration span may be very short. You will need to decide whether to play one round of a game or more. Adapt the games as you play them, and don't feel you have to play them in exactly the same way every time. It's often better to make up your own variations and rules.

Instructions for each game appear under the equipment lists, and on the opposite page you will find some ideas for extending or varying the game, sometimes for older or more mature children sometimes to refresh the game when you know it well and have played it often.

Many of the games are suitable for children to play on their own with one or two friends, after they have been shown how to play them by an adult. Children could also take maths games home as part of a toy library or as an alternative to story bags or language games.

The Songs and Rhymes

The songs and rhymes in the book are varied in content, origin and intended use:

▶ some are old favourites – counting rhymes and number songs

▶ some songs have new words sung to familiar tunes

▶ some rhymes are new versions of old favourites, renewed by the emphasis on numbers and counting

▶ some rhymes and songs are intended for use as you play the games.

5

Links with the Early Learning Goals for the Early Years Foundation Stage

Most of the Early Learning Goals have links with some part of the maths curriculum. The following goals are particularly relevant to playing maths games and singing number songs:

Personal and Social Development:
- be confident to try new activities, initiate ideas and speak in a familiar group;
- work as part of a group or class, taking turns and sharing fairly, understanding that there need to be agreed values and codes of behaviour for groups of people, including adults and children, to work together harmoniously.

Communication, Language and Literacy:
- interact with others, negotiating plans and activities and taking turns in conversations;
- listen with enjoyment and respond to stories, songs, and other music, rhymes and poems and make up their own stories, rhymes and poems.

Problem Solving, Reasoning and Numeracy:
- say and use number names in order in familiar contexts;
- count reliably up to 10 everyday objects;
- recognise numerals 1-9;
- use developing mathematical ideas and methods to solve practical problems;
- in practical activities and discussion begin to use the vocabulary involved in addition and subtraction;
- use language such as more, less, to compare two numbers;
- find one more or one less than a number from 1-10;
- begin to relate addition to combining two groups of objects, and subtraction to taking away;
- use language such as greater, smaller, heavier or lighter to compare quantities;

- use everyday words to describe position;
- talk about, recognise and recreate simple patterns;
- use language such as 'circle', or 'bigger' to describe the shape and size of solids and flat shapes;
- use developing mathematical ideas and methods to solve practical problems.

Knowledge and Understanding of the World:
- look closely at similarities, differences, patterns and change.

Physical Development:
- move with control and co-ordination;
- use a range of small and large equipment.

Creative Development:
- sing simple songs from memory, recognise repeated sounds and sound patterns and match movements to music;
- use their imagination in art and design, music, dance, imaginative and role play and stories.

Each page in this book indentifies the relevant goals for the activity described.

Pass it On

Focus: Counting 1-6

What you need

- small items such as bears, beads, coins, nuts
- a number or dotty dice 1 - 6 or 1 - 5
- four children

You need quite a lot of these items for 'Pass it on'. You can mix the items or have all the same.

What you do

1. Each player takes 10 items. Help them to count them out or let them help each other.
2. Choose a starting player.
3. The starting player rolls the dice, says that number on the dice and then gives the number of their items to the player on their left.
4. Pass the dice to the player on the right.
5. Continue until one player has given away all their items.

You could also play until one player has 20 items.

Variations...

▶ Play the game with sand or water. Each player has a small bowl of sand or water and a spoon.

They throw the dice and give the right number of spoonfuls to the person on their left. Play until one bowl is empty.

Links with EYFS goals

PSD – work as part of a group taking turns and sharing fairly.
CLL – interact with others.
PSRN – say and use number names in order in familiar contexts; count reliably up to 10 everyday objects; use developing mathematical ideas and methods to solve practical problems;
PD – move with control and co-ordination; use a range of small and large equipment.

'Here we go Round the Number Ring'

A song to sing to 'Here we go Round the Mulberry Bush'

Here we go round the number ring,
The number ring, the number ring,
Here we go round the number ring,
Passing to each other.

How many things have you got now?
Have you got now, have you got now?
How many things have you got now?
Passing to each other.

We can pass the water round,
The water round, the water round,
We can pass the water round,
Passing to each other.

Splat that Number

Focus: Number recognition (best outside!)

What you need

- a washing line and pegs
- number cards from 1 - 10 (or 1 - 5) laminated or in small zip lock bags
- balls, bean bags or bats and balls
- chalk
- a whiteboard or clipboard and pen
- four children

If you laminate the number cards the children can play the game outside all the year round.

What you do

1. Peg the numbers on the line (in order or random).
2. Chalk a line on the ground about two metres from the washing line.
3. Choose a starting player.
4. The starting player takes a ball or bean bag and throws it at the line. They score the number they hit, if they can say it.
5. Put the score on the board or take the number off the line.
6. Continue until everyone has had two turns.
7. The winner is the person who has scored the most in two turns.

For younger children, have one turn each and the winner starts the next game. Move the line back for older or more mature children.

Variations...

▶ Chalk the numbers on a wall or fence and use wet sponges to score.

▶ Draw numbered circles on the ground and toss bean bags into them.

▶ Paint numbers on buckets and toss balls or bean bags into them to score.

Links with EYFS goals

PSD – be confident to try new activities, initiate ideas and speak in a familiar group

PSRN – say and use number names in order in familiar contexts; recognise numerals 1 - 9

PD – move with control and co-ordination; use a range of small and large equipment.

'Ten Little Numbers'

A song to sing to the tune of Ten Green Bottles

Ten little numbers hanging on the line,
Ten little numbers hanging on the line,
And if one little number blows down off the line,
There'll be nine little numbers hanging on the line.

Nine little numbers hanging on the line
and so on...

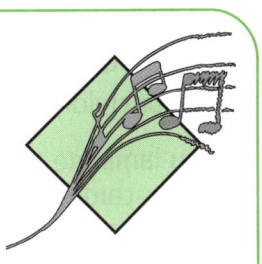

Find the Shape

Focus: Shape

What you need

- a feely bag or box. You can make a feely box from a carton with a hole cut in the side. For a feely bag use a fabric shoe bag, or make a simple bag and label it.
- pairs of shapes or objects with a clear shape
- two children

You can use plastic shapes (2D or 3D), plastic fruit, beads, small bricks, small world vehicles, etc.

What you do

1. Display one set of shapes where the children can see them clearly.
2. With the bag hidden, put one of the shapes inside and give the bag to one child.
3. The child must feel the object and find its pair from the ones they can see. If they are right they keep the shapes.
4. Continue until all the pairs have been found.

Start with a small number of pairs and give the children plenty of time to feel inside the bag.

Variations...

▶ Put an object in the bag. The player must describe the object (not just name it).

▶ Put several shapes in the bag. Hold up one 'twin' shape. The player must find its pair by touch alone.

▶ Put several shapes in the bag. Describe the shape you want. The player must find the pair by touch alone.

Links with EYFS goals

PSD – be confident to try new activities, initiate ideas and speak in a familiar group; work as part of a group or class, taking turns and sharing fairly.

PSRN – use language such as 'circle', or 'bigger' to describe the shape and size of solids and flat shapes.

CD – respond with all their senses.

'The Feely Box'

A rhyme to learn

If you feel in the feely bag (or box),
what will you find?

Toys or shapes, bricks or fruit,
We don't mind.

We feel in the feely box and guess what's there,
Soft or hard, square or round,
We don't care.

We feel in the feely box and say what we've found,
We use our fingers as our eyes
And look without a sound.

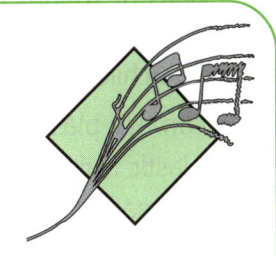

Play that Number

Focus: Counting/beat

What you need

- ▶ a selection of instruments (drum, tabor, triangle, chime bar)
- ▶ beaters
- ▶ number cards 1 to 5 or 1 to 10
- ▶ four children

Start with a choice of two instruments and use those which can be beaten with a hand. A beater adds another thing to think about!

What you do

1. Sit in a circle on the carpet or round a small table.
2. Put the cards face down in a pile in the middle.
3. The first child chooses an instrument.
4. You (or a child) turn over the first number card.
5. The player must play that number of beats on their instrument. The other players count the beats. The first player says the number and keeps the card if they are right.
6. Pass the instrument to the player on the right.
7. Continue until all the cards are gone.

The rest of the group could clap as the player plays the beat

Variations...

- Each child has an instrument. The first player plays the number, then the passes it to the next person round the ring.
- One child plays a number of beats, another child finds the matching card.
- Turn over two or three cards and play the sequence.
- Turn over a card and play 'one more' or 'one less' beat.

Links with EYFS goals

PSD – work as part of a group or class.

CLL – listen with enjoyment and respond to music, and make up their own music.

PSRN – say and use number names in order in familiar contexts.

PD – use a range of small and large equipment.

CD – recognise repeated sounds and sound patterns and match movements to music.

'We Can Count with the Tambourine'

A song to sing to the tune of 'We Can Play on the Big Bass Drum.'

We can count on the tambourine,
And this is the way we do it,
One two three on the tambourine,
And this is the music to it.

We can count on the triangle,
And this is the way we do it,
One two three on the triangle,
And this is the music to it.

We can count on the maraccas,
And this is the way we do it,
One two three on the maraccas,
And this is the music to it... and so on

15

Junk Numbers

Focus: Number recognition

What you need

- ▶ junk mail, catalogues and magazines
- ▶ scissors
- ▶ glue sticks
- ▶ paper
- ▶ four children

Collect junk mail from all your friends and encourage parents and children to bring theirs in too. Old equipment catalogues are really useful, so collect some from exhibitions and shops.

What you do

1. Each player takes an item of junk mail, a pair of scissors and a glue stick.
2. Look at the junk mail together and talk about the difference between numbers, letters and pictures. Find places where numbers are – prices, page numbers, sizes, order forms, phone numbers.
3. When you say 'go', the players race to find, cut and stick the numbers from 0 to 5 or 0 to 10 – in the right order!
4. The winner is the first to collect and stick the numbers.

Younger children may need to tear the numbers.

Variations...

▶ Find as many 3s (or another number) as they can. Cut and stick them.

▶ Collect numbers of pictures – eg. faces, cars, toys, hands, wheels. You could draw a circle on each child's paper and write the number to remind them.

▶ Race against a timer or stop watch.

Links with EYFS goals

PSD – work as part of a group or class.

CLL – listen with enjoyment and respond to music, and make up their own music.

PSRN – say and use number names in order in familiar contexts; count reliably up to 10 everyday objects; recognise numerals 1-9.

PD – use a range of small and large equipment.

A new version of 'One Finger, One Thumb'

A song to sing while you work

One finger, one thumb keep moving,
One finger, one thumb keep moving,
One finger, one thumb keep moving,
One finger, one thumb keep moving,
We're cutting numbers out.

One finger, one thumb, one hand keep moving,
One finger, one thumb, one hand keep moving,
One finger, one thumb, one hand keep moving,
One finger, one thumb, one hand keep moving,
We're spreading on the glue.

One finger, one thumb, one hand in a fist keep moving,
One finger, one thumb, one hand in a fist keep moving,
One finger, one thumb, one hand in a fist keep moving,
One finger, one thumb, one hand in a fist keep moving,
We're sticking the numbers down.

Through the Arches

Focus: Number (good for outside)

What you need

- a strong cardboard box
- scissors or craft knife
- paint or a felt pen
- one car, truck, or small ball for each player
- playground chalk
- a clipboard and pen
- two, three or four children

This game can have any numbers over the arches. You decide the numbers the children need to practise.

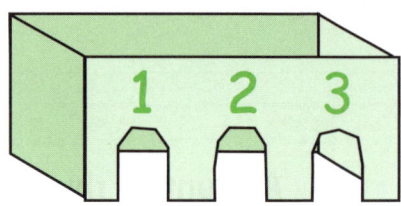

What you do

1. Get the children to help you to make the arches. Cut the top and bottom out of the box. Cut some arches with a knife or scissors (adult only!). Make as many arches as you like.
2. The children can decorate the box and paint or write the numbers over each arch.
3. Chalk a starting line on the ground.
4. The players take a car or ball each and roll them towards the arches.
5. Write the score for each player. Have another go and find a winner.

Variations...

▶ Use an arches box without numbers to help very young children with hand control.

▶ Make a game with 6 or 10 arches. Each player has two (or three) balls or cars. Take turns to roll both balls, then total the score.

▶ Cut circular holes in the top of a box. Play by tossing beanbags through the holes.

Links with EYFS goals

PSD – work as part of a group or class, taking turns and sharing fairly.

CLL – interact with others.

PSRN – say and use number names in order in familiar contexts; count reliably up to 10 everyday objects; recognise numerals 1-9; use everyday words to describe position.

PD – use a range of small and large equipment.

'Ten Little Cars'

A counting rhyme to say

Ten little racing cars parked in a line,
One drove away and then there were nine.
Nine little racing cars drove through the car park gate,
One had lost his ticket and that left eight.
Eight little racing cars on a journey down to Devon,
One got lost and then there were seven.
Seven little racing cars doing driving tricks,
One bumped into a lamp post and then there were six.
Six little racing cars set off on a drive,
One got lost and then there were five.
Five little racing cars making tyre tracks on the floor,
One got a puncture and then there were four.
Four little racing cars on a visit to the sea,
One got stuck in the sand and then there were three.
Three little racing cars on a mountain with a view,
One slid to the bottom and that left two.
Two little racing cars were parked in the sun,
One went fast asleep and that left one.
One little racing motor car, having so much fun,
Drove into his garage and that left none.

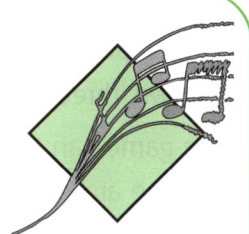

Big Races

Focus: Counting on

What you need

- ▶ a large flat surface (a table, board or floor space)
- ▶ large sheets of strong white paper
- ▶ masking tape or big clips
- ▶ thick felt pens
- ▶ play people or other items for playing pieces
- ▶ large dice
- ▶ any number of children

It's useful for children to have experience of playing other race games before making their own.

What you do

1. Tape or clip the paper firmly to the table or other surface. Masking tape works well on floors and paving slabs
2. Talk with the children about race games. Look at some examples and talk about how they work. Choose a theme for your game (race to the castle, round the zoo, to the moon).
3. Draw a track for the game. The track should not be numbered for the first game you make. Let the children do as much as they can and don't try to make it perfect!
4. Colour and decorate the game before you play.
5. Throw the dice and count the squares as you play.

Variations...

▶ Make a new game and include some forfeits or tasks. Try things like this – 'Stand up, turn round, sit down', 'Clap three times', 'Sing a nursery rhyme', 'Count backwards from 10'.

▶ Make the game on a sheet of plastic using paint with glue in it. This will last much longer.

Links with EYFS goals

PSD – be confident to try new activities; work as part of a group or class.

PSRN – say and use number names in order in familiar contexts; count reliably up to 10 everyday objects.

PD – move with control and co-ordination.

CD – use their imagination in art and design.

'Count to Five'

A song to sing, to the tune of 'Twinkle, Twinkle, Little Star'

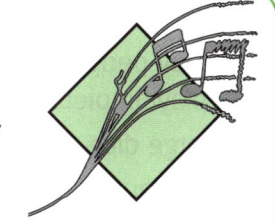

One and two and three and four,
I can count and count some more,
Five and six, seven, eight, nine, ten,
Now I can count back again
Ten, nine, eight, seven, six five, four,
Three and two and then one more.

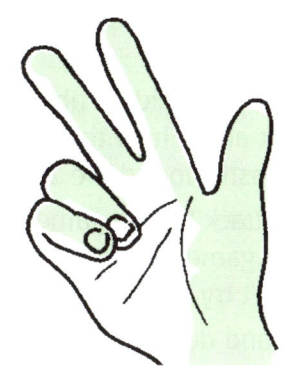

Grab and Guess

Focus: Estimation

What you need

- a jar, small basket or other container with a wide opening
- small items such as beads, coins, dried pasta or small bricks
- a small container/bowl for each player
- laminated number cards
- four children

You need quite a lot of these items for 'Grab and Guess'. You can mix the items or have all the same. Keep the items quite big to start with.

What you do

1. Put the items in the big container.
2. Choose a starting player.
3. The first player grabs a handful of things from the container and puts them on the table. They guess how many, then count. If they are right, they put the things in their own bowl; if not, they put them back.
4. Continue until everyone has had several goes.
5. The winner is the player with the most items in their bowl.

You could have tokens for each right guess instead of keeping the items.

Variations...

▶ After they count, the player must find the correct number card for their guess.

▶ Make the game more difficult by using smaller items such as dried beans, peas, coins or counters.

▶ Use a feely bag and get the children to estimate without looking (a hard game!)

Links with EYFS goals

PSD – be confident to try new activities.
CLL – interact with others.
PSRN – say and use number names in order in familiar contexts; count reliably up to 10 everyday objects; recognise numerals 1-9.
PD – move with control and co-ordination; use a range of small and large equipment.

'Grab and Guess'

A song to sing to the tune of 'Hot Cross Buns'

Grab and guess,
Grab and guess,
First you guess and then you count,
Grab and guess.

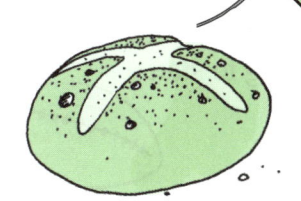

And another song to sing to the tune of 'I Hear Thunder'

We are guessing,
We are guessing,
You guess too, you guess too,
It doesn't matter if you're wrong,
Give a guess now, come along,
You guess too,
You guess too.

Button Toss

Focus: Counting 0-6 or 0-10; writing numbers

What you need

- some large flat buttons, any colour (about 10)
- paint (with some white glue added) – any single colour
- recording sheets like this
- four children

The buttons can be different sizes and shapes, but they all need to be flat, and the bigger the better. Charity shops or grandparents are good sources of buttons!

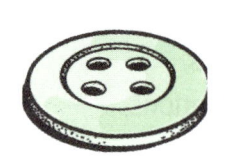

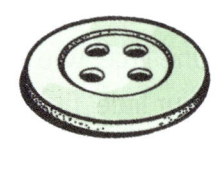

0	1	2	3	4	5
			3		

What you do

1. Involve the children in painting the buttons on one side only. Leave them to dry.
2. Use five buttons for less experienced players, 10 (or more) for more experienced counters.
3. The first player takes all the buttons and tosses them on the table. They count the buttons which fall coloured side up, and record that number in the right column on the record sheet.
4. Play continues. The winner is the first to get the same number three times.

Less experienced players may need help with the recording.

Variations...

▶ Play the game with dried butter beans painted in the same way.

▶ Paint some beans or buttons in two or three colours. Record how many of each fall face up, using two or more columns on the sheet.

▶ Before you throw, guess how many will fall coloured side up.

Links with EYFS goals

PSD – be confident to try new activities; work as part of a group or class, taking turns and sharing fairly.

CLL – interact with others.

PSRN – say and use number names in order in familiar contexts count reliably up to 10 everyday objects; recognise numerals 1-9; use developing mathematical ideas and methods to solve practical problems.

'The Button Song'

A song to sing to the tune of 'One Little, Two Little, Three Little Indians'

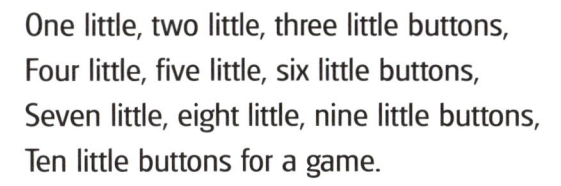

One little, two little, three little buttons,
Four little, five little, six little buttons,
Seven little, eight little, nine little buttons,
Ten little buttons for a game.

How many buttons will be red ones?
How many buttons will be red ones?
How many buttons will be red ones?
How many buttons will be red ones?
When we toss them into the air.

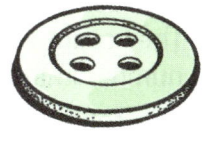

Spot the Dots

Focus: Pattern, memory and counting

What you need

- ▶ some small items, large dice or dot cards
- ▶ a small cloth or bowl to cover the items you are using
- ▶ raisins
- ▶ four children

Children need to play this game with real things before they move to dots or cards.

It's easier to count quickly if the items are identical (small bricks, buttons, compare bears, etc).

What you do

1. The game leader puts several items under the cloth or bowl.
2. Say a player's name, then remove the cover briefly before putting it back.
3. The player must hold up the correct number of fingers and say the number of dots or items.
4. Remove the cover and count together.
5. If the player is right they take a raisin to eat.

Remember, younger children need more time.

Variations...

▶ Play the game with dominoes and count the spots.

▶ Play the game again using number cards or fans. The player must hold up the correct number as they say it.

▶ Use bigger numbers of things, or a mixture of things under the cover for more mature children.

Links with EYFS goals

PSRN – say and use number names in order in familiar contexts; count reliably up to 10 everyday objects; recognise numerals 1-9; use developing mathematical ideas and methods to solve practical problems.

K&U – look closely at similarities, differences, patterns and change.

'This Old Man, He Played One'

This old man, he played one,
He played knick knack on my drum,
With a knick knack paddiwack,
Give the dog a bone,
This old man came rolling home.
This old man, he played two,

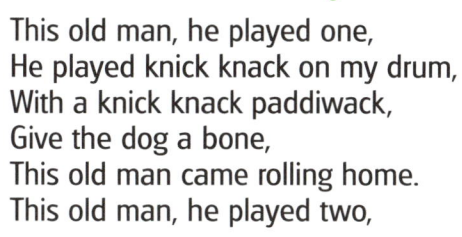

He played knick knack on my shoe,
With a...etc.

This old man, he played three,
He played knick knack on my tree,
With a...etc.

This old man, he played four,
He played knick knack on my door,
With a ..... etc.

This old man, he played five,
He played knick knack on my drive,
With a...etc.

Under the Cup

Focus: Subtraction

What you need

- ▶ yogurt pots or plastic cups
- ▶ small items such as beans, bears and counters
- ▶ any number of children

Children need to recognise the concept of less or take away for this game. Play it without the cup first, so they know what's happening.

What you do

1. Count some items into the cup.
2. Say 'I'm taking out (or 'I'm putting in')... more.' Then turn the cup upside down. Start by adding or taking one thing until the children are familiar with the game.
3. The children hold up the right number of fingers for the number now under the cup.
4. When the children are familiar with the game, they can take a turn with the cup and be game leader.

Exaggerate your movements for the youngest children.

Variations...

▶ You can either ask individuals or the whole group to respond.
▶ Play the game using number cards or fans for responses.
▶ Remove more than one item or put mixed items under the cup.
▶ Put a number line on the table and get the children to point to the new number.

Links with EYFS goals

PSD – be confident to try new activities;
PSRN – count reliably up to 10 everyday objects; recognise numerals 1-9; use developing mathematical ideas and methods to solve practical problems; in practical activities and discussion begin to use the vocabulary involved in addition and subtraction; use language such as 'more', 'less', to compare two numbers.

'The Busy Workmen'

A number rhyme

One busy workman digging a hole,
Two busy workmen putting up a pole,
Three busy workmen piling up bricks,
Four busy workmen clearing mud and sticks,
Five busy workmen building a high wall,
Six busy workmen playing football,
Seven busy workmen shovelling some sand,
Eight busy workmen giving them a hand,
Nine busy workmen see it's half past three,
Ten busy workmen have a cup of tea.

Skittles

Focus: Counting 1-6 or 1-10

What you need

- 6 or 10 empty plastic bottles - from milk, squash or water
- sand and a funnel
- paint with glue mixed in
- permanent markers
- white glue
- children to help
- chalk
- a soft ball
- a score board

(a whiteboard, clip board or flip chart)

This game needs careful preparation.

What you do

The children can do all the stages of this!

1. Paint the bottles all over with a single colour. Leave to dry.
2. When dry use a range of colours to make patterns on the bottles. Leave to dry again.
3. When dry, put about 5cm of sand in the bottom of each bottle.
4. Put glue inside the tops and screw them on tightly.
5. Paint a number on each bottle.
6. To play the game, set the bottles up, draw a starting line and take turns to roll the ball. Write the scores on the board.
7. Roll once each. The winner is the player with the highest score after a set number of goes.

Variations...

▶ Play the game with three balls. Each player has three rolls to knock down as many bottles as possible.

▶ Make a miniature game with small water bottles to play indoors.

▶ Older children may be ready to play in teams of one or four scoring for the team.

Links with EYFS goals

PSD – work as part of a group or class, taking turns and sharing fairly;

CLL – interact with others, negotiating plans and activities and taking turns in conversations.

PSRN – count reliably up to 10 everyday objects; recognise numerals 1-9; in practical activities and discussion begin to use the vocabulary involved in addition and subtraction.

PD – move with control and co-ordination.

A rhyme to say as you play
'Roll a Ball'

Roll a ball, roll a ball,

Knock the skittles down.

Can you score a jackpot

By knocking them all down?

Write your score, write your score,

Write it on the board.

Don't forget to put your name

By the number you have scored.

Roll a ball, roll a ball,

Knock the skittles down.

Can you score a jackpot

By knocking them all down?

Hide and Find

Focus: Recognising numbers 1-6 or 1-10

What you need

- ▶ plastic or wooden numbers (several of each numeral)
- ▶ one of the following in a bowl or deep tray – sand, water, gloop, compost, cooked pasta, cornflour, jelly or cellulose paste
- ▶ a big number dice
- ▶ two or three children

You can make a big dice from a box covered in paper or a play brick with numbers written on.

What you do

Have fun finding numbers in tactile materials, either using a dice or calling out a number. Start with 1 – 3 then 1 – 6. Before you start, bury or mix the numerals in the bowl with the sand, etc. Make sure you have enough to cover the numbers completely.

2. Roll the number dice. The children say the number, then dig to find it.
3. If you use water, you can fish with nets for the numbers.
4. Children can keep or return the numbers once they have caught and named them. If they keep them, and the new number has already been collected, roll the dice again.

One child can roll and call the numbers if you like.

Variations...

▶ Give the children a water proof number line to match the numbers as they find them.

▶ Play the game in the garden. Before you play, go out and hide the numerals in bushes and trees and under stones and leaves. Use hoops or baskets to collect each number.

Links with EYFS goals

PSD – be confident to try new activities.

PSRN – say and use number names in order in familiar contexts; count reliably up to 10 everyday objects; recognise numerals 1-9.

CD – respond with all their senses.

'The Helpers'

A counting rhyme

One busy helper closing the door.

Two busy helpers sweeping the floor.

Three busy helpers putting bikes away.

Four busy helpers empty the water tray.

Five busy helpers hang the aprons on their hooks.

Six busy helpers tidy all the books.

Seven busy helpers put away the toys.

Eight busy helpers, what helpful girls and boys.

Nine busy helpers, tidying the house.

Ten busy helpers sitting quiet as a mouse.

Well done!

Lotto

Focus: Number recognition

What you need

- ▶ Lotto tickets (like the ones here) and pencils or pens
- ▶ a plastic bowl for the balls (a salad spinner is really good for this!)
- ▶ ping pong balls
- ▶ permanent marker
- ▶ pencils
- ▶ four children

Make the Lotto cards with the appropriate range of numbers to match the children's stage of Problem Solving, Reasoning and Numeracy.

0	3	1
2	5	4

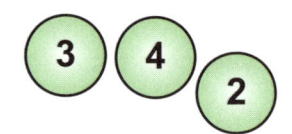

What you do

1. Make some tickets. You could make ones with more numbers when children are ready for them.
2. Mark each ping pong ball with a number from 0-6 or 0-10 (or higher if the children can recognise the numbers).
3. Every player has a Lotto ticket.
4. The caller (an adult until the children are used to the game) takes one ball at a time out of the bowl and says the number.
5. Players cross out the number if it is on their Lotto ticket.
6. Continue until one player has crossed out all their numbers. They must shout 'Lotto' when they have filled their ticket.

One child can roll and call the numbers if you like.

Variations...

- Use pictures or dots on the cards and numbers on the balls.
- Use really big numbers when older or more mature children can cope with them.
- Play outside with two big lotto cards chalked on the ground, footballs with numbers and children to cover the numbers as they are taken out out.

Links with EYFS goals

PSD – work as part of a group or class, taking turns and sharing fairly.

CLL – listen with enjoyment.

PSRN – say and use number names in order in familiar contexts; count reliably up to 10 everyday objects; recognise numerals 1-9.

'Lotto'

A song to sing to the tune of 'Frere Jacques'

Playing lotto, playing lotto,

Hope I win, hope I win.

See the balls go round and round,

Bouncing up and falling down.

Take one now, take one now.

Playing lotto, playing lotto,

Hope I win, hope I win.

If it's there you cross it out,

Take a pencil, cross it out.

Who will win, who will win?

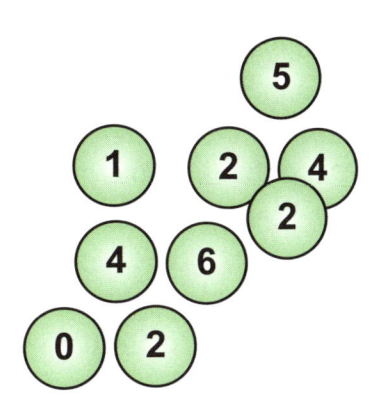

Turn Two, Match Two

Focus: Number (or shape, money)

What you need

- ▶ Lotto tickets (like the ones here) and pencils or pens
- ▶ a plastic bowl for the balls (a salad spinner is really good for this!)
- ▶ ping pong balls
- ▶ permanent marker
- ▶ pencils
- ▶ four children

Make the Lotto cards with the appropriate range of numbers to match the children's stage of Problem Solving, Reasoning and Numeracy.

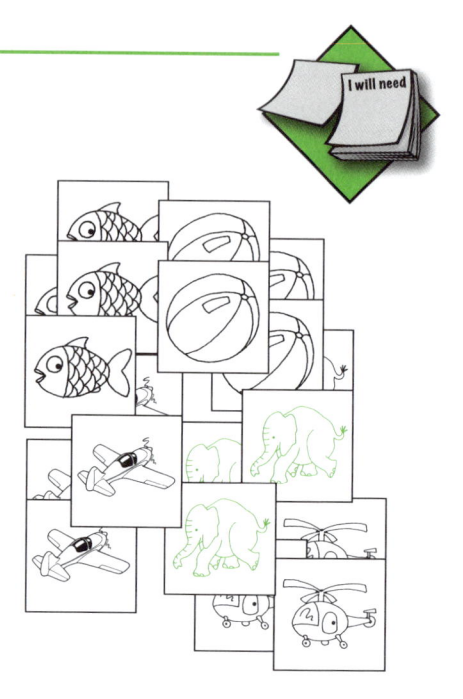

What you do

1. Make your sets of cards (the children could help) and talk about them with the children. Always show the pictures to the children first, to allow them to 'key in' to the pictures, before playing.
2. Put the cards face down on the table or floor.
3. Take turns to pick two cards. If they match, keep them. If not, put them back exactly where they came from.
4. The winner is the person with the most cards at the end of the game.

Make several sets of cards so you can vary the game; you could copy the pictures on page 68.

Variations...

- Play pairs with pairs of real objects, such as animals, cars, dinosaurs, etc., hidden in sand or in a feely bag.
- Use pictures the children have drawn, scanned into the computer and printed small. You could also use digital photos of the children in your group, by printing two of each.

Links with EYFS goals

PSD – work as part of a group or class, taking turns and sharing fairly.

CLL – interact with others, negotiating plans and activities and taking turns in conversations.

PSRN – use everyday words to describe position; talk about, recognise and recreate simple patterns.

K&U – look closely at similarities, differences and patterns.

'One Two'

A traditional counting rhyme

One two, buckle my shoe,

Three, four, knock at the door,

Five, six, pick up sticks,

Seven, eight, lay them straight,

Nine, ten, a big fat hen.

Eleven, twelve, dig and delve,

Thirteen, fourteen, maids a courting,

Fifteen, sixteen, maids in the kitchen,

Seventeen, eighteen, maids a-waiting,

Nineteen, twenty, my plate's empty.

Big Numbers

Focus: Counting 1-6 or 1 - 20

What you need

- ▶ playground chalk or masking tape
- ▶ a large flat surface indoors or in the garden
- ▶ children

You could mark this square permanently on the path or even on the floor inside. A big square piece of carpet can easily be made into a number square by painting the grid with gloss paint or using a spray can and stencils.

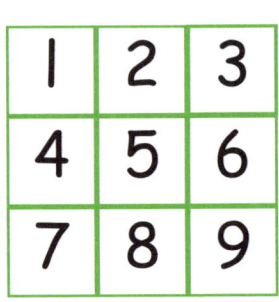

1	2	3
4	5	6
7	8	9

1	2	3	4	5
6	7	8	9	10
11	12	13	14	15
16	17	18	19	20

What you do

Before you start this game, mark the number square on the floor or ground with chalk, paint or masking tape. Get the children to help you if possible. Make the individual squares as big as possible. Start with a 1 to 9 square (as above).

Game 1. Take turns to jump on the squares in turn, saying the number as you go

Game 2. You call a number and the children run to stand on it.

Game 3. Toss a bean bag onto the square and write the number on a white board. Take two turns each and see who wins.

Game 4. Get some small toys and put one on square 1, two on square 2, and so on.

Variations...

- Make a more permanent square on carpet, plastic or fabric.
- Make the number square bigger as the children learn more numbers.
- Play 'Whole Body Race to 20' or 50 or 100 with playground dice. You will need to throw the dice for them as they jump their way along the numbers.

Links with EYFS goals

PSD – be confident to try new activities; work as part of a group or class.

CLL – interact with others, negotiating plans and activities.

PSRN – say and use number names in order in familiar contexts; recognise numerals 1-9; use everyday words to describe position.

PD – move with control and co-ordination.

'Big Numbers'

A counting rhyme

We can count in tens you know,
This is how it needs to go,

Count in tens up to one hundred,
Count with us and then you'll know.

Ten, twenty, thirty, forty, fifty,
Sixty, seventy, eighty, ninety, one hundred.

Count in tens along with us,
We will show the way to you.

Count in tens up to one hundred,
Now you know big numbers too.

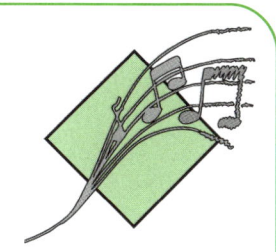

10, 20, 30, 40, 50, 60, 70, 80, 90, 100

Only Two More Days

Focus: Counting on and counting backwards

What you need

This is a good activity for the beginning of a new month or term

- large piece of paper
- some calendars and diaries to look at
- highlighters and felt pens
- four children at a time, or the whole class if you want to make a class calendar

Make your calendar on big sheets of paper with plenty of space for writing and pictures of the events on each day or using a spray can and stencils.

What you do

1. Talk with the children about calendars and diaries, look at some together and talk about birthdays and other special days. Let them help you to make a week or a month's calendar page on a big piece of paper.
2. Now mark the weekend days and the school/nursery days, and any special events such as birthdays, outings, festivals. The children can draw pictures and write the numbers.
3. Now play 'first to find' – a day, an event, a visit. Start at the visit and count back to today, start at today and count how many days until the event. Display the calendar and look at it every day.

Variations...

- Make a whole year calendar and mark birthdays and events in advance.
- Use the same calendar and involve the children in recording a picture for each day after it has happened – a pictorial diary on a calendar!
- Put diaries and calendars in the role play areas.

Links with EYFS goals

CLL – interact with others, negotiating plans and activities; listen with enjoyment and respond to rhymes and poems.

PSRN – say and use number names in order in familiar contexts; use developing mathematical ideas and methods to solve practical problems.

K&U – look closely at similarities, differences, patterns and change.

'The Months of the Year'
A calendar poem

January brings the snow,
Makes our feet and fingers glow.

February brings the rain,
Thaws the frozen ponds again.

March brings breezes loud and shrill,
Stirs the dancing daffodil.

April brings the primrose sweet,
Scatters daisies at our feet.

May brings flocks of pretty lambs,
Skipping by their fleecy dams.

June brings tulips, lilies, roses,
Fills the children's hands with posies.

Hot July brings cooling showers,
Strawberries and gilly flowers.

August brings the sheaves of corn,
Then the harvest home is borne.

Warm September brings the fruit,
Sportsmen then begin to shoot.

Fresh October brings the pheasant,
Then to gather nuts is pleasant.

Dull November brings the blast,
Then the leaves are falling fast.

Chill December brings the sleet,
Blazing fire and Christmas treats.

by Sara Coleridge

Let's Pretend

Focus: One to one, more and less, matching

What you need

Play these games in your role play area or at a table with a cloth

- four or five sets of plastic plates, cups, saucers, spoons, etc.
- food items (real or imitation)
- number cards
- four children

You could use dried pasta, big beans, nuts or other natural objects or use salt dough and bake biscuits, sausages, burgers, fruit, etc.

What you do

Role play is a really good place for games.

1. Sit round the table and look at the things you have prepared.
2. Play 'How much food do you want?' taking turns to serve the right number of objects to the person on your left. They then serve the person on their left. Model the sorts of numbers to match the children's stage of development.
3. Now play 'Take one, take two.' Start with all the food on one plate and practise taking a number (you could put a pile of number cards face down in the middle of the table).
4. Play 'Sharing out' – take turns to count out a bowl of pasta shapes or biscuits so everyone has the same number.

Variations...

- Play 'One More, One Less'. Players take turns to ask another person to give them one more or one less than a number e.g. 'Give me one less than five cakes'.
- Make repeating food patterns (with fake food) eg jam tart, bun, jam tart, bun or or with pasta shapes or letters.

Links with EYFS goals

PSD – work as part of a group or class, taking turns and sharing fairly.

PSRN – in order in familiar contexts; count reliably up to 10; in practical activities and discussion begin to use the vocabulary involved in addition and subtraction; find one more or one less than a number from 1-10.

CD – use their imagination in role play.

'Serving'

A song to sing to the tune of 'Wind the Bobbin'

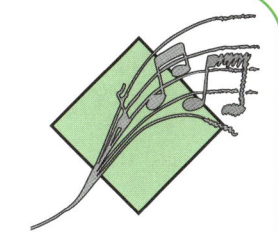

Serve the pasta out, serve the pasta out.
One, two, three, four, five.
Serve the spoonfuls out, serve the spoonfuls out.
One, two, three, four, five.

One on the red plate, one on the blue,
One for me and one for you;
One on the yellow plate, one on the green,
This is the best pasta you've ever seen!

Snap a Shape

Focus: 2D shapes

What you need

- shape cards
- four children

Use the shapes at the end of the book to make a set of shape snap cards. If you colour them before you cut them out (or let the children do it), you will be able to play more complex games with colour and shape matching at the same time.

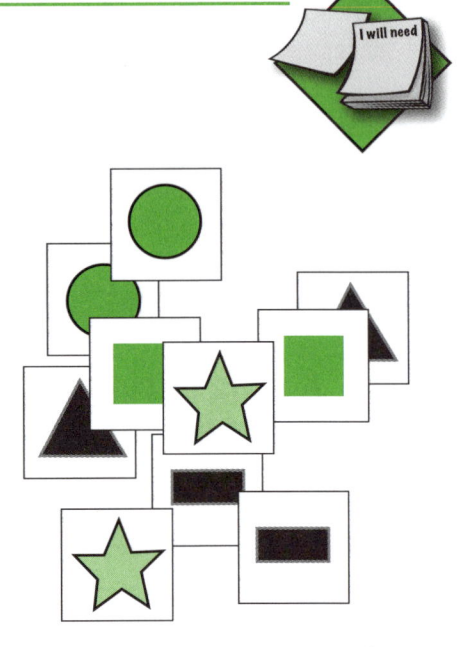

What you do

1. Talk to the children about the shapes and the game before you start. Start with 20 cards and five shapes (four of each).
2. Deal the cards out, so everyone has the same number.
3. The first player puts a card down face up.
4. The next player puts a card down on top of the first. If it matches, the first to shout the name of the shape wins both cards, and puts them at the bottom of their pile.
5. Continue until one player has collected all the cards.

Some children find it easier to see the snaps if you make two piles of cards.

Variations...

- Play pairs with the same cards by putting them face down on the table and turning over two at a time to get pairs.
- Play 'Snap a Coin' with coin cards or 'Snap a Picture' with picture cards.
- Use a feely box or bag to play 'Snap a Shape' with 2D shapes.

Links with EYFS goals

PSD – work as part of a group or class, taking turns and sharing fairly.

PSRN – use language such as circle, or bigger to describe the shape and size of solids and flat shapes.

CD – look closely at similarities, differences, patterns and change.

'Finding Pairs'

A song to sing to the tune of 'Twinkle, Twinkle, Little Star'

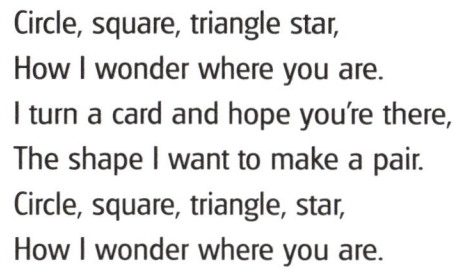

Circle, square, triangle star,
How I wonder where you are.
I turn a card and hope you're there,
The shape I want to make a pair.
Circle, square, triangle, star,
How I wonder where you are.

'Count in Twos'

Count your cards along with me,
I can count in two you see,
It's not all that hard to do,
You help me and I'll help you,
2, 4, 6, 8, count with me,
I can count to twenty!

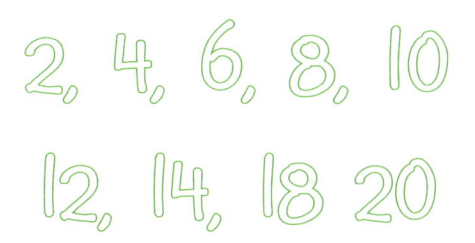

2, 4, 6, 8, 10
12, 14, 18 20

Penny Exchange

Focus: Money and counting

What you need

- a large number of 1p coins (plastic or real)
- smaller numbers of 2p, 5p and 10p coins
- number dice, 1 to 6 or 1 to 5
- four children

You need a lot of coins for this game, and real ones are always better so children to get used to the feel of money.

What you do

Game 1. Players take turns to toss the dice and take the number of 1p coins on the dice.
Pass the dice to the next player
Play three rounds.
The winner is the child with the most coins at the end of three rounds.

Game 2. Play game 1 and at the end, each player must exchange their 1p coins for 2p or 5p or 10p coins.

Game two is only suitable for children who understand the difference between 1p and 2p!

Variations...

▶ Label some little zip lock bags with different numbers. Children must put the right amount of money in each bag. Start with small amounts and pennies before adding 2p, 5p, 10p coins.

▶ Make some cards with prices from junk mail. Use them to play a coin matching game.

Links with EYFS goals

PSD – be confident to try new activities; work as part of a group or class.

PSRN – count reliably up to 10 everyday objects; recognise simple coins.

K&U – look closely at similarities, differences, patterns and change.

CD – sing simple songs from memory.

'The Penny Game'

A song to sing as you play, to the tune of 'Frere Jacques'

Your turn (Jamie), your turn (Jamie),
Throw the dice, throw the dice,
Now you count the pennies out,
Now you count the pennies out,
Keep them safe, keep them safe.

(Continue round the circle until everyone has had three turns)

Now we count them, now we count them,
Who has won? Who has won?
Count and see who's got the most,
Count and see who's got the most,
Now who's won? Now who's won?

(Now congratulate the winner, clapping as you sing)

Well done (Carly), well done (Carly),
You have won, you have won,
(Carly) won the game this time,
Carly won the game this time,
Let's play again! Let's play again!

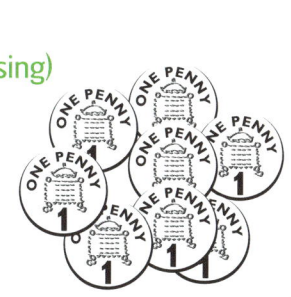

Button Your Coat

Focus: Counting 1-6

What you need

- some coat cards (see picture)
- real buttons (they don't need to match but they do need to fit on the card coat)
- number or dotty dice 1 to 6
- four children

You could adapt this game by making cards for apples on trees, fish in ponds, petals on flowers etc. Wrapping paper is a good source of pictures, and charity shops are a good source for buttons.

What you do

Make the cards with six or seven buttons for less experienced counters, then move on to ten, twelve and even twenty for the more advanced counters in your group.

1. Each player has a coat card.
2. Take turns to throw the dice and take the right number of buttons. Put these on your card.
3. Pass the dice to the player on the left.
4. The first player to fill all their buttons wins the game.
5. Play again with the winner starting.

Once they know what to do, even the youngest children can play this game on their own.

Variations...

▶ Make a big collaborative version of this game – it could be a spotty dog, an apple tree or a bunch of flowers. Make spots, apples or flowers and stick Velcro on back and on the picture.

▶ Photocopy some random button patterns and make them into matching or counting games.

Links with EYFS goals

PSD – work as part of a group or class, taking turns and sharing fairly.

PSRN – say and use number names in order in familiar contexts; count reliably up to 10 everyday objects.

PD – move with control and co-ordination; use a range of small equipment.

'Button Up'

A song to sing to the tune of 'Twinkle, Twinkle, Little Star'

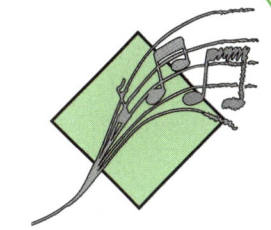

Play this game called 'Button Up',
With coat and card and buttons and cup.
Roll the dice and count the dots.
Put the buttons on the spots.
Count the buttons, one, two, three.
Pass the dice along to me.

Up the Ladder

Focus: Counting

What you need

- a big sheet of card or thick paper
- felt pens or chalk
- counters, cars or small world people for markers
- a 2p coin
- four children

You can play this game outside by making a track or ladder on the path or playground. Draw it with chalk or powder paint – they wash off in the rain.

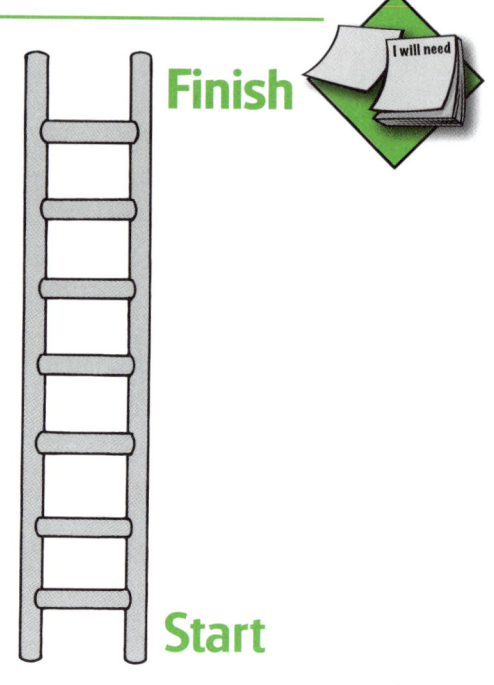

Finish

Start

What you do

Get the children to help you make the track or ladder, using felt pens or chalk. The track can be any length. Don't put numbers on it.

1. Each player chooses a marker object.
2. Choose a starting player and a number from 1 to 5.
3. The first player tosses the coin. If it lands 'heads' up, they move the number of steps agreed for the game. If it lands 'tails' up, they stay where they are.
4. Pass the coin to the next player.
5. Continue until one player reaches the end of the track.

Variations...

- Make a really big ladder and play with soft toys as playing pieces.
- Make small ladders and laminate them for pairs of children to play together.
- Paint a big ladder on the path in the garden so children can make up their own games.

Links with EYFS goals

CLL – interact with others.

PSRN – say and use number names in order in familiar contexts; count reliably up to 10 everyday objects; recognise numerals 1-9; use language such as 'more' and 'less', to compare two numbers; find one more or one less than a number from 1-10; use everyday words to describe position.

'Up the Ladder'

A song to sing to the tune of 'Boys and Girls Come out to Play'

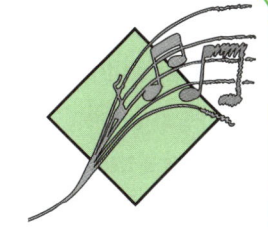

Boys and girls come out to play,
Make a game, we'll show you the way,
Get some card and get some pens,
And we'll climb the ladders, with all our friends.

You bring pens and I'll bring card,
And we'll make a game, it won't be hard,
Come with a penny, to have a go,
And we'll practise counting so we'll all know.

Boys and girls come out to play,
Make a game, we'll show you the way,
Get some card and get some pens,
And we'll climb the ladders, with all our friends.

Hop, Skip and Jump

Focus: Counting

What you need

- musical instruments with a clear beat e.g. a drum, tabor, triangle, chime bar, maraccas
- beaters
- big number cards
- movement pictures (e.g. jump, hop, stamp, clap)
- any number of children

Using the whole body for counting helps children to develop the steady beat necessary for accurcy.

What you do

Practise following a beat in a big space, maintaining the steady beat as children walk, jump, hop, clap. When they can follow a continuous steady beat, try these games:

Game 1. The adult plays a number of beats and the children follow, moving any way they want.

Game 2. The adult chooses a movement and then plays the phrase. The children must remember the number of beats and the movement.

Game 3. The adult holds up a number, says a movement and the children follow, counting each beat

Game 4. A child is the leader, playing and counting.

Variations...

- Each child has an instrument. One person (adult or child) plays and moves. The others follow.
- One player plays a number pattern, the others must echo it on their instruments.
- One player models a movement and holds up a card. Others echo the movement and play the beat.

Links with EYFS goals

PSD – work as part of a group or class.

CLL – listen with enjoyment and respond to music.

PSRN – say and use number names in order in familiar contexts; count reliably up to 10 everyday objects.

PD – move with control and co-ordination.

CD – recognise repeated sounds and sound patterns and match movements to music.

'Keep it Moving'

A song to sing to 'London's Burning'

Keep it moving, keep it moving,
Clap your hands, clap your hands,
Follow my beat, follow my beat,
Keep it moving, keep it moving.

Keep it moving, keep it moving,
Stamp your feet, stamp your feet,
Follow my beat, follow my beat,
Keep it moving, keep it moving.

Keep it moving, keep it moving,
Slap your legs, slap your legs,
Follow my beat, follow my beat,
Keep it moving, keep it moving.

and some more movements for more verses:

Blink your eyelids, shrug your shoulders, pat your tummy, click your fingers and wriggle your noses

Number Spot

Focus: Number recognition 0-9

What you need

- number cards 0 to 9, or scrap card or paper
- crayons
- playing boards (see illustration)
- four children

This game is just about numbers, so make sure the children can recognise all the numbers before playing the game.

| 0 | 1 | 2 | 3 | 4 |
| 5 | 6 | 7 | 8 | 9 |

What you do

Explain the game clearly before you begin.

1. Cut or tear the scrap paper into 20 pieces and write the numbers 0-9 on the pieces. You will have enough for two of each.
2. Mix up the number cards and put them in a pile, face down.
3. Every player needs their own playing board and a crayon.
4. Players take turns to take a number card. They find the number on their own card and colour it in.
5. If they turn up a number they have already coloured, they miss a go.
6. Continue until one player has coloured all their numbers.

Variations...

▶ Make some playing boards on white boards with permanent markers, so that children can play the game on their own with dry wipe colouring.

▶ Extend the game to 0-20 for those children who can cope with bigger numbers.

Links with EYFS goals

PSRN – say and use number names in order in familiar contexts; count reliably up to 10 everyday objects; recognise numerals 1-9.

PD – use a range of small and large equipment.

'Ten Little Teddies'

A counting rhyme to learn

Ten little teddies hanging on the line,
One fell off and that left nine.
Nine little teddies swinging on the gate,
One went in the garden and that left eight.
Eight little teddies looking up to heaven,
One tripped over and that left seven.
Seven little teddies building with some bricks,
One went to ride his bike and that left six.
Six little teddies go to swim and dive,
One went to sunbathe and that left five.
Five little teddies standing by the door,
One didn't want to came so that left four.
Four little teddies paddling in the sea,
One went to dry his feet and that left three.
Three little teddies off to the zoo,
One was scared of elephants so that left two.
Two little teddies lying in the sun,
One went to fetch his hat and that left one.
One little teddy sitting all alone,
He went to find his mum and that left none.

Go Fish!

Focus: Counting 1-6

What you need

- ▶ a bowl or water tray and water
- ▶ a thin sponge sheet that you can cut out
- ▶ permanent markers
- ▶ small fishing nets
- ▶ small bowls or buckets
- ▶ four children

This is a very wet game! Make sure you have protected surfaces and children, or play it outside.

What you do

1. Cut about 10 fish from the foam sheet. Draw eyes and fins, and draw a different number of dots on each fish. Start with 1 to 5.
2. Float the fish in the water.
3. Take turns to catch a fish with a net and put it in your bowl.
4. When all the fish have been caught, each player lays out their catch and counts the dots.
5. The winner is the player with the most dots at the end of the game.

You could put the number as well as the dots on the fish.

Variations...

▶ Make a magnet fishing game with card fish. Cut out and decorate the fish. Put numbers or dots on each.
Clip a paper clip on the nose of each fish, and put them in a bowl or empty aquarium. Fish with small rods made from garden sticks with string and a small magnet attached.

Links with EYFS goals

PSD – work as part of a group.

CLL – interact with others; listen with enjoyment and respond to rhymes and poems.

PSRN – say and use number names in order in familiar contexts; count reliably up to 10 everyday objects; recognise numerals 1-9.

PD – use a range of small and large equipment.

'One, Two, Three, Four, Five'

A traditional song to sing

One, two, three, four, five.
Once I caught a fish alive,
Six, seven, eight, nine, ten,
Then I let it go again.

Why did you let it go?
Because it bit my finger so.
Which finger did it bite?
This little finger on the right.

Step and Squeeze

Focus: Counting 1-10 (or more) on and back

What you need

- some scrap paper or card
- thick felt pens
- double sided tape or Blutack
- ten hoops or chalk circles on the ground
- a home made dice with 'on' and 'back' written on (see picture)
- four children

If you have some card, this will last longer. You could cut sides from cereal boxes and write on the back.

What you do

You need ten (or more) pieces of paper or card. Write one number on each (the children could do this), and put each one in a hoop or circle. You need room in the circle for more than one child.

1. Choose a starting player. Roll the dice. If it says 'ON' the player moves on one number and says the number as s/he lands. If it says 'BACK' s/he moves back one number and say the number when landing. The player stays on the number till their next turn.
2. Take turns to roll the dice and move along the hoops.
3. The winner is the first person to reach ten.

If there is more than one player in the hoop, they must help each other to stay there! If you fall out you go back to 1.

Variations...

- ▶ Make a dice with 'ON', 'BACK' and 'STAY' and play again.
- ▶ Play the game with soft toys. Each player has a soft toy and moves it along the track.
- ▶ Paint a permanent version on the path in the garden and leave a different dice out each week for the children to play independently.

Links with EYFS goals

PSD – work as part of a group or class, taking turns and sharing fairly.

PSRN – say and use number names in order in familiar contexts; recognise numerals 1-9; in practical activities and discussion begin to use the vocabulary involved in addition and subtraction; use everyday words to describe position.

PD – move with control and co-ordination.

'Step and Squeeze'

A song to sing to the tune of 'Here We Go Round the Mulberry Bush'

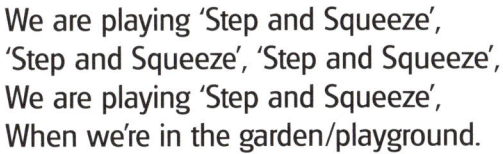

We are playing 'Step and Squeeze',
'Step and Squeeze', 'Step and Squeeze',
We are playing 'Step and Squeeze',
When we're in the garden/playground.

First you have to throw the dice,
Throw the dice, throw the dice,
First you have to throw the dice,
When you're in the garden.

Then you hop or jump or step
On or back, on or back,
Then you hop or jump or step
When you're in the garden.

When you meet you have to squeeze,
You have to squeeze, you have to squeeze,
When you meet you have to squeeze,
When you're in the garden.

Think of a Number

Focus: Recognising and ordering numbers

What you need

- ▶ some number lines from 0 to 10
- ▶ a set of single number cards from 0 to 10
- ▶ crayons
- ▶ four children

Make the first number lines big enough for children to see and point to numbers clearly.

What you do

1. Each player has a number line.
2. Put the number cards in a pile, face down.
3. The caller (an adult to start with) takes the first card and says 'I am thinking of a number between X and X.' For example if they took 3, 'I am thinking of a number between 1 and 5.'
4. The other players must guess which number it is. When they have guessed correctly, the caller turns the number card round and all players colour in that number on their line,
5. Continue until all the cards have been used.

This is the collaborative version where everyone wins!

Variations...

▶ Take turns to guess. Each player has three goes to guess the number in turn. You will need more number cards for this, because the player keeps the card if they guess the number.

▶ Use longer number lines, as children get more confident.

▶ Let the children take a turn as caller.

Links with EYFS goals

PSRN – say and use number names in order in familiar contexts; recognise numerals 1-9; find one more or one less than a number from 1-10.

PD – use a range of small and large equipment.

'Counting Backwards'

A song to sing to the tune of 'I hear Thunder'

Lets count backwards,
Lets count backwards,
You count too,
You count too,
10, 9, 8, 7, 6, 5, 4,   (you need to say this bit fast
10, 9, 8, 7, 6, 5, 4,   to fit in with the music!)
3, 2, 1,
3, 2, 1.

10, 9, 8, 7, 6, 5, 4, 3, 2, 1

In The Hoop You Go!

Focus: Sorting

What you need

- a pack of playing cards
- two or three hoops (or ropes tied at the ends)
- paper and a felt pen
- four or more children

You can use playing cards for all sorts of games. Here is one.

Red cards only

What you do

Start with one hoop on the floor. Decide what you are going to collect in the hoop. Make a label for the hoop. It could say '10' or 'red cards only', or 'picture cards' or 'hearts', etc.

1. Deal all the cards round the group. Each player puts their pile face down in front of them.
2. Take turns to turn over one card. If it fits in the hoop, put it in. If not, make another pile with the discards.
3. Continue until all the cards have been turned.
4. If you want a winner, count how many cards each player has left. The one with least cards wins.

You could play with half a pack to start with.

Variations...

A game for older children

▶ Play the game with two hoops, overlapped like this:

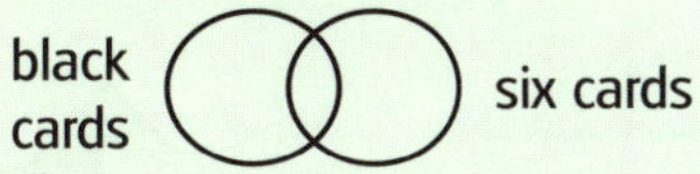

black cards   six cards

Play as before, but talk about where a black six card might go to be in both hoops. Try with different combinations and even three hoops (e.g. red, picture, clubs)
* this is really difficult!

Links with EYFS goals

PSRN – say and use number names in order in familiar contexts; recognise numerals 1-9; find one more or one less than a number from 1-10.

PD – use a range of small and large equipment.

A song to sing while sorting

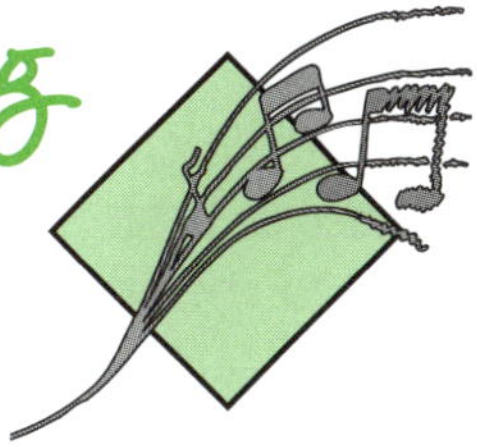

(Change the words if you are sorting counters, Lego, pasta, teddies, etc.)

Red and yellow, pink and blue,
Sorting buttons, me and you.
Sort the colours, sort the size,
Sort the shapes, just use your eyes.
Pick them up and you will see
You can sort them easily.
All you need are buttons and pots,
Lots of buttons, lots of pots.
Help your friend to write the label
For each pot, if you are able.
Stick the labels on the pots,
Now get buttons, you need lots.
Sort them out and you will see,
You can sort them easily.

P.S. You can colour uncooked pasta by putting some in a zip lock bag with a few drops of food colouring, rolling them around, then drying them on a tray or newspaper.

Blindfold!

Focus: Counting 1-6 or 1-10

What you need

- small items such as bears, beads, coins, nuts
- a soft scarf for a blindfold (you could use a sports sweatband if it is soft enough for eyes
- two or three children

The items need to be small enough for children to hold several in their hand, but not too small to count! If in doubt try it yourself – just shut your eyes and try to hold and count ten of the objects.

What you do

1. Take turns to be blindfold.
2. One child chooses some objects and puts them in the blindfold child's hands.
3. The blindfold child counts the objects and says the number. If they are right, they keep those objects.
4. Continue to take turns to be blindfold. There is no winner for this game, just praise for taking risks!

This game takes some getting used to. Some children hate having their eyes covered, so give them plenty of opportunity to do this in play situations first, for example by putting blindfolds in the role play area.

Variations...

- Use a blindfold instead of a feely box for a change.
- Use blindfolds and plastic or wooden numerals to make up another game.
- Play 'Pick Up'. A blindfold player has to pick up a number of objects named by another player.

Links with EYFS goals

PSD – be confident to try new activities, initiate ideas and speak in a familiar group

PSRN – say and use number names in order in familiar contexts; count reliably up to 10 everyday objects use developing mathematical ideas and methods to solve practical problems.

PD – move with control and co-ordination.

CD – use all of their senses.

'Counting Blindfold'

A song to sing to the tune of 'In and Out the Dusty Bluebells'

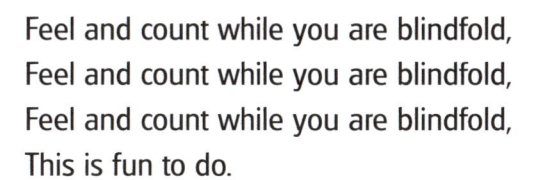

Feel and count while you are blindfold,
Feel and count while you are blindfold,
Feel and count while you are blindfold,
This is fun to do.

You must count them without peeping,
You must count them without peeping,
You must count them without peeping,
It is fun to do.

If you count them, you can keep them,
If you count them, you can keep them,
If you count them, you can keep them,
Then perhaps you'll win!

Button Sort

Focus: Counting 1-6

What you need

- a collection of buttons of different sizes, colours and shapes
- some plastic trays or small shallow boxes
- picture/word clue cards – see page opposite
- four children

Fruit or vegetable trays from supermarket packs are ideal for this game. Avoid those which have been used for meat, and take care with polystyrene.

What you do

1. Look at the buttons and talk about sizes, shapes and colours. Each player chooses ten buttons.
2. Put the cards face down on the table.
3. Choose a starting player. He or she chooses one of their buttons and puts it in the middle of the table.
4. The next player turns over a card and looks at the clue. They choose one of their buttons to match the clue card, and put it next to the first button. Everyone checks to see if they are right.
5. Continue to take turns until one player has no buttons left.

Variations...

▶ Once they get used to it, children can play this game on their own or in pairs without an adult.

▶ Play the same game with sticky paper shapes and stick the sequence down.

▶ Play with other small objects such as cars, counters, beads.

Links with EYFS goals

PSRN – use developing mathematical ideas and methods to solve practical problems; use everyday words to describe position; talk about, recognise and recreate simple patterns; use language such as 'circle', or 'bigger' to describe the shape and size of flat shapes.

K&U – look closely at similarities, differences, patterns and change.

Sample clue cards for Button Sort

Copy these cards and colour them, or make your own to match your button collection.

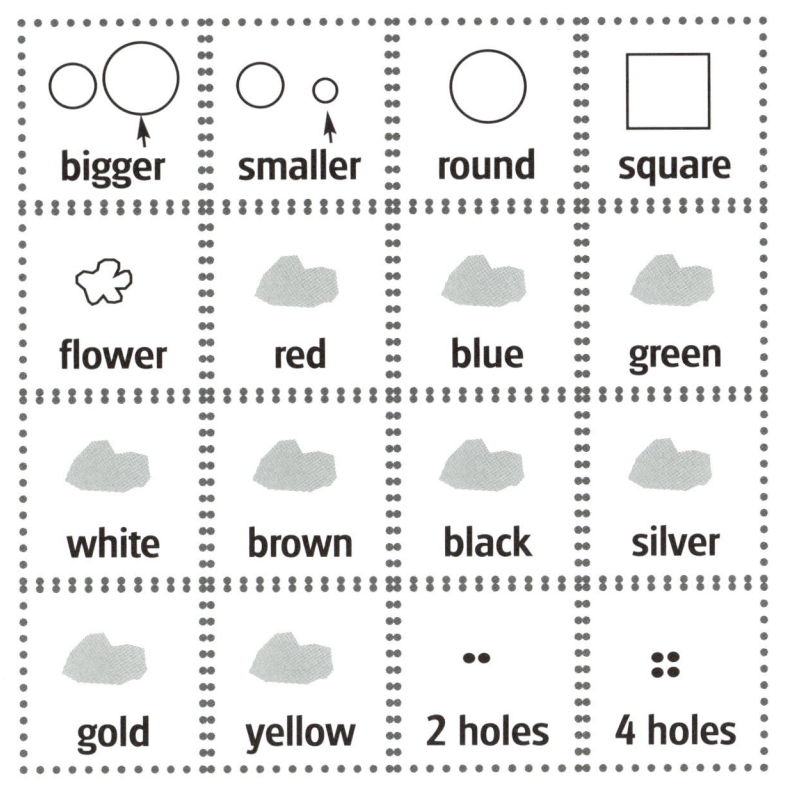

bigger	smaller	round	square
flower	red	blue	green
white	brown	black	silver
gold	yellow	2 holes	4 holes

67

Some pictures for a Pairs Game

Coins to photocopy for games and challenges

Shapes

The Little Books Club

There is always something in Little Books to help and inspire you. Packed full of lovely ideas, Little Books meet the need for exciting and practical activities that are fun to do, address the Early Learning Goals and can be followed in most settings. Everyone is a winner!

We publish 5 new Little Books a year. Little Books Club members receive each of these 5 books as soon as they are published for a reduced price. The subscription cost is £37.50 – a one off payment that buys the 5 new books for £7.50 instead of £8.99 each.

In addition to this, Little Books Club Members receive:
- Free postage and packing on anything ordered from the Featherstone catalogue
- A 15% discount voucher upon joining which can be used to buy any number of books from the Featherstone catalogue
- Members price of £7.50 on any additional Little Book purchased
- A regular, free newsletter dealing with club news, special offers and aspects of Early Years curriculum and practice
- All new Little Books on approval - return in good condition within 30 days and we'll refund the cost to your club account

Call 020 7440 2446 or email: littlebooks@acblack.com for an enrolment pack. Or download an application form from our website:

www.acblack.com/featherstone

The **Little Books** series consists of:

- All Through the Year
- Bags, Boxes & Trays
- Bricks and Boxes
- Celebrations
- Christmas
- Circle Time
- Clay and Malleable Materials
- Clothes and Fabrics
- Colour, Shape and Number
- Cooking from Stories
- Cooking Together
- Counting
- Dance
- Dance, with music CD
- Discovery Bottles
- Dough
- 50
- Fine Motor Skills
- Fun on a Shoestring
- Games with Sounds
- Growing Things
- ICT
- Investigations
- Junk Music
- Language Fun
- Light and Shadow
- Listening
- Living Things
- Look and Listen
- Making Books and Cards
- Making Poetry
- Mark Making
- Maths Activities
- Maths from Stories
- Maths Songs and Games
- Messy Play
- Music
- Nursery Rhymes
- Outdoor Play
- Outside in All Weathers
- Parachute Play
- Persona Dolls
- Phonics
- Playground Games
- Prop Boxes for Role Play
- Props for Writing
- Puppet Making
- Puppets in Stories
- Resistant Materials
- Role Play
- Sand and Water
- Science through Art
- Scissor Skills
- Sewing and Weaving
- Small World Play
- Sound Ideas
- Storyboards
- Storytelling
- Seasons
- Time and Money
- Time and Place
- Treasure Baskets
- Treasureboxes
- Tuff Spot Activities
- Washing Lines
- Writing

All available from
www.acblack.com/featherstone